Heinrich Schmidbauer and Hans Joachim Wieland

Making Hidden Tang Knives

4880 Lower Valley Road, Atglen, Pennsylvania 19310

Other Schiffer Books on Related Subjects:

The Lockback Folding Knife: From Design to Completion,
 978-0-7643-3509-9, $29.99

Basic Knifemaking: From Raw Steel to a Finished Stub Tang Knife,
 978-0-7643-3508-2, $29.99

Making Integral Knives,
 978-0-7643-4011-6, $29.99

Making Knife Sheaths, Vol. 1,
 978-0-7643-4015-4, $29.99

Originally published as *Steckangelmesser, Schritt für Schritt: Vom rohen Stahl zum fertigen Messer mit Scheide* by Wieland Verlag GmbH
Translated by Ingrid Elser and John Guess
Cover design and layout by Caroline Wydeau; Photos by Hans Joachim Wieland

Schiffer Books are available at special discounts for bulk purchases for sales promotions or premiums. Special editions, including personalized covers, corporate imprints, and excerpts can be created in large quantities for special needs. For more information contact the publisher:

Schiffer Publishing Ltd.
4880 Lower Valley Road
Atglen, PA 19310
Phone: (610) 593-1777; Fax: (610) 593-2002
E-mail: Info@schifferbooks.com

For the largest selection of fine reference books on this and related subjects, please visit our website at **www.schifferbooks.com**

We are always looking for people to write books on new and related subjects. If you have an idea for a book, please contact us at proposals@schifferbooks.com

This book may be purchased from the publisher. Include $5.00 for shipping. Please try your bookstore first. You may write for a free catalog.

In Europe, Schiffer books are distributed by
Bushwood Books
6 Marksbury Ave.
Kew Gardens
Surrey TW9 4JF England
Phone: 44 (0) 20 8392 8585; Fax: 44 (0) 20 8392 9876
E-mail: info@bushwoodbooks.co.uk
Website: www.bushwoodbooks.co.uk

Copyright © 2012 by Schiffer Publishing, Ltd.
Library of Congress Control Number: 2011944410

Revised Design by Stephanie Daugherty
Type set in Courier Std/Frutiger LT Std

ISBN: 978-0-7643-4014-7
Printed in China

CONTENTS

A FEW WORDS UP FRONT

Knifemaking as a hobby is becoming increasingly popular. More and more people are discovering how much joy it can be to create such a pretty yet practical device on their own. The start into this hobby is usually a fixed blade. It is far easier to construct than a folder because it doesn't have any moving mechanisms. Nevertheless, a fixed blade also poses its challenges to the knifemaker—all the more if you construct the blade yourself and don't use manufactured blades.

There are two different ways to construct a fixed blade: either the knife has a flat tang to which the handle scales are attached laterally. Or it has a hidden tang upon which the handle is put. This volume of the workshop series deals with the second type, which is more demanding and quite often more aesthetic.

We filed the blade manually because most beginning knifemakers don't have a belt sander. Also, pure manual work has its charm—not only for the knifemaker, but for the potential customer who perhaps purchases the knife later on. For some people only a manually filed knife is a truly handmade knife. Filing is strenuous, but it is also fun and evokes a special feeling of satisfaction with respect to the finished knife.

With this workshop series we aim to help you with all technical questions and spare you quite a few errors. This series of books presents a variety of knifemaking themes in a step-by-step approach that you can follow by yourself. We especially emphasize the usability of these volumes in the workshop. Thus all the volumes have a wire binding so the book stays open when you put it down on the workbench. Also, we made sure that the images and fonts are big enough to see when the book is lying next to you as you work.

This volume is based on several workshop articles which were published in the German periodical *Knife Magazine (Messer Magazin)*. The material was revised and updated, and we have tried to explain every step in the most comprehensive way. But before you pick up your tools, you should read through the descriptions and explanations in this book first. This way you'll know what to expect and won't be confronted with unpleasant surprises later on.

I wish you fun and success with your work!

Hans Joachim Wieland
Chief Editor, *Messer Magazin (Knife Magazine)*

The handmade knife is one of mankind's oldest tools. Even today, a period characterized by technology and industry, the knife has not lost any of its fascination and importance. Just the opposite—modern humans increasingly try to escape from the daily routine, which is determined by machines. More and more people are on the search for the simple and basic things in life. They remember and realize the value of craftsmanship and natural materials. A knife in its simple, authentic shape gives back part of the things that are essential to us all.

A knife can have a soul. A prerequisite for this is the knifemaker himself/herself. He/She is the person who gives life to the steel. The knifemaker spends many hours of effort on constructing a knife. He/She uses their own hands and through them the knife receives its soul.

This is also linked to perfection: you have to invest the time necessary to give the knife its final polish in accordance with the motto, "If you think your knife is finished, then work on it for another hour!"

There are different reasons to begin knifemaking. Since I am a hunter, I wanted to buy a high-quality knife in a Nordic style that met my needs. But I didn't find anything like this on the market. So I decided to construct my own knife. This was anything but easy and I encountered many setbacks. But I was driven by ambition. I was lucky to come in contact with very good knifemakers who voluntarily answered my questions and also gave me moral support. So, my first usable hunting knife came into being.

My biggest problem at the beginning was the blade. I didn't want a manufactured blade, but a blade of my own with the shape I wanted. For this, the blade has to be carved from a piece of steel. My first knives were all filed by hand. At that time I didn't have a belt sander. The only machine I used was a drill press.

My experience was that of many newbies. Some cut their teeth with a manufactured blade. But this should really only be the beginning, as training for handling the materials and tools. I feel that true knifemakers construct blades of their own!

With lots of diligence and perseverance, success will come, too. There are lots of colleagues who are willing to give precious tips to beginners. Seek the conversation! But be aware: Once you've started with knifemaking, it may become an addiction—one that is hard to get away from.

Heinrich Schmidbauer

INTRODUCTION

Essentially, there are two ways to construct a fixed blade: the hidden tang and the full tang method. With a hidden tang knife, the tang is hidden inside the handle—as the name implies. Here the tang is a thin, round or rectangular extension of the blade. With a full tang knife, the tang is flat and in general of the same thickness as the back of the blade. The handle consists of two parts which are mounted to the left and right. In between, the tang usually stays visible and reaches up to the handle butt.

Two paths towards the same goal: above, a full tang knife shaped like a traditional Bavarian hunting knife made by the company Lindner of Solingen, Germany; below, a hidden tang knife created by Heinrich Schmidbauer.

Photo: Linder

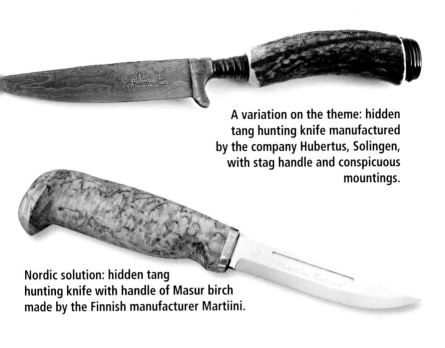

A variation on the theme: hidden tang hunting knife manufactured by the company Hubertus, Solingen, with stag handle and conspicuous mountings.

Nordic solution: hidden tang hunting knife with handle of Masur birch made by the Finnish manufacturer Martiini.

Both ways of production have traditional roots. They possess various advantages and disadvantages. A full tang knife has somewhat simpler production and a tendency toward higher stability. In contrast, the hidden tang has aesthetic advantages, especially with respect to handles with a round profile. In addition, with these knives you only touch the handle material, not the steel, which makes them a little more pleasurable to handle than full tang knives.

This volume deals with hidden tang knives exclusively. This kind of construction is typical for a multitude of traditional knife forms e.g. the classic Bavarian hunting knife or the Finnish puuko. Especially in Scandinavia, hidden tang knives are by far the preferred knives, which has something to do with the temperature in this area during the winter. At low temperatures, well below 0°F, handles made of horn, bone, or leather with a hidden tang are "warmer" to the hand than a full tang knife with edges of cold steel accessible from the sides.

With a hidden tang knife, the handle is either simply put on and glued, or the handle end is screwed on or riveted. With handles that are simply put on, the tang can reach more or less far inside the handle. Here this general rule applies: The farther the tang reaches into the handle, the more stable the construction. A special kind of construction is used for Japanese samurai swords: Here the handle is put on and then secured with a perpendicular bamboo bolt which is pushed through a hole in the tang.

The difficulty with respect to a hidden tang knife lies in producing an exact fit between handle and tang. This requires a proper procedure, some manual dexterity, and, above all, lots of patience. In general, to check the fit you have to mount the knife many times, take it apart again, refine it, assemble it again, and so on. Whoever takes this effort is rewarded with a beautiful and solid result.

American Classic: Hidden tang knife made by the company Randall with a handle that combines stag horn and leather with brass mountings and spacers made from brass and vulcanized fiber.

The photos in this volume were taken at Heinrich Schmidhauer's workshop. This well-known knifemaker demonstrated to us all the steps of his work by means of practical examples. Fixed blade knives with hidden tangs are Heinrich Schmidbauer's signature knife style. He has lots of experience with this type of knife and offers valuable and practical tips.

We documented all the different steps in knifemaking (designing the blade, producing and etching it, adding the handle, and making the sheath) for various knives. But this doesn't matter because the underlying construction and basic design are identical. This manual is not meant to enable you to reproduce a specific knife, but to let you understand the concept and each single working step so you will be able to build any hidden tang knife. With this knowledge you can work freely with your own designs and let your creativity run wild.

The working steps and procedures shown here are meant as a suggestion. We don't have a monopoly on wisdom and also don't claim to know the one and only saintly method. Many ways lead to Rome, and there are a lot of different ways which lead to the same result. Other knifemakers surely work in a different way to Heinrich Schmidbauer with respect to details. Find out what works best for you and work along these lines.

THE TOOLS

All work steps are intentionally done with the simplest tools possible. The blade is filed manually, and you won't need a big machine shop, just basic workshop equipment. The only machine that you will need is a drill press. In a pinch, a stand on which you can mount your hand drill is also sufficient, but nowadays every home improvement store has decent drill press machines for a fair price. For the drill press you will also need a small vise to clamp in your work pieces for drilling.

Beyond that, it is recommended that you get a small variety of high-quality files. Besides buying flat files in various sizes and cuts (see more about this on the opposite page), you should get several round files and at least one mill saw file (with smooth edges). Look for quality: The file is the knifemaker's most important tool, and a good file lasts a long time.

The most important tool of any knifemaker: Files with different profiles and cuts.

GRADES OF CUT AND THEIR MEANING

Depending on their length, files of the same cut have different cut numbers. The number of cuts per centimeter for Swiss-pattern files is approximately:

Swiss-pattern Cut Number	American Pattern Equivalent	Tooth Number (Teeth per centimeter)
0	—	4.5 - 10
1	Bastard	5.3 - 16
2	Second Cut	10 - 25
3	Smooth Cut	14 - 35
4	—	25 - 50
5	—	40 - 71

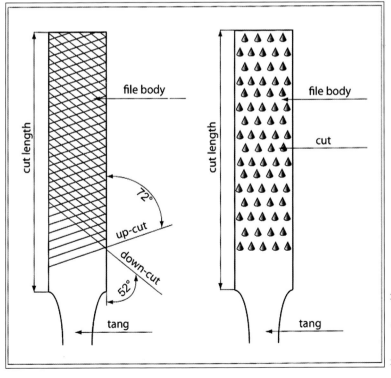

Graphic: Peter Fronteddu

Another essential tool is a proper vise. A rather heavy vise is recommended because there is nothing worse than a wobbly vise! A practical addition is a holding device that you can clamp the knife in and turn if necessary. You can build such a device yourself, or purchase one ready made (see image below).

Equally important is a wide range of abrasive cloth and sandpaper. In general, both are the same; the abrasive grain is just applied on a different basic material. Especially coarse grit can usually be obtained as cloth, fine grit is mostly based on paper. Abrasive cloth is more robust and thus lasts longer. For coarse work you start with grit P120, than you continue via P180, 240, 320, and 400 up to the fine grits P600 and P800. For an especially fine finish you can also use P1200.

Very flexible and practical: Professional holding device for knives made by Frank Wojtinowski. It can be clamped in the vise and turned in all directions.

No substitute for these: Abrasive cloth and sandpaper with various grits as well as battens or sanding blocks for achieving a level surface.

When working with sandpaper, but also with the file, the following applies: Always work with ascending grits and always work in 90° angles. The marks from sanding with the next, finer grit should be perpendicular to the marks left over from the previous work step. This way you will be sure to remove all grooves and prevent the creation of waves within the surface. Only change to the next finer grit after the marks of the previous work step have been completely removed.

Another quite practical tool is a scribing block—an apparatus that holds a scriber at adjustable heights. This will allow you to make horizontal scribing lines, e.g. to mark the centerline on the edge of the blade. In a pinch, you can also use a wing divider to scribe the line twice, once from each side. This way you can see deviations from the center and are able to correct them accordingly. Also very helpful for scribing is layout dye, which you apply to the blade so the scribed line is more visible.

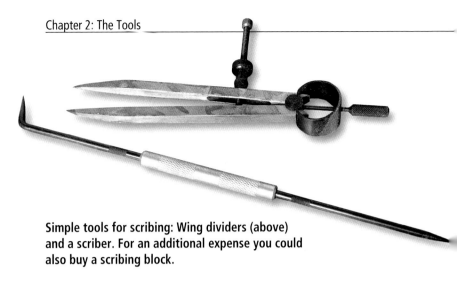

Simple tools for scribing: Wing dividers (above) and a scriber. For an additional expense you could also buy a scribing block.

Anything else you need should be available in most home improvement and hobby shops: Different drill bits for metal and wood, metal and wood saws, felt pens, pencil, hammer, awl, center punch, tongs, and a few screw taps. For etching the blade (when using a Damascus steel blade) you need an appropriate receptacle and the necessary acid (more about this in chapter 5). For constructing the leather sheath you need a shoemaker's knife for cutting and a harness needle for sewing, in addition you need an adjustable groover and perhaps a bone folder. More about this in chapter 7.

A multitude of possibilities exists for the final sharpening of the blade. Here, Heinrich Schmidbauer is working with a diamond file. With this tool it is relatively easy to take away the final fractions of material from the hardened edge.

Finally, a word about safety: As with every hobby related to craftsmanship, there are also risks to your health in knifemaking. Even if you are mainly working with manual tools, not machines, you can nevertheless badly injure yourself. So please always be careful, work calmly and with concentration, and protect yourself with proper protective clothes. Always wear protective goggles because metal particles will fly off very fast when drilling, grinding, milling, and welding.

In addition, many materials pose hidden dangers: Dust from sanding wood, bone, or ivory can be poisonous and can accumulate in your lungs. Protect yourself by wearing a respirator while filing and sanding.

Working with solvents, adhesives, and acids, your work place should be well ventilated. If possible, move your operation outdoors where you breathe in the least amount of vapors.

Don't let these protective measures take away your joy at work. It is important to think about these issues and to act accordingly. After all, knifemaking should be fun and may develop into a hobby that you pursue for many years.

TOOLS

- vise (with felt jaws or special holding device)
- drill press with vise
- various files
- abrasive cloth, grit P180-800
- drill bits for steel
- drill bits for wood
- waterproof felt pen
- pencil
- ruler
- layout dye
- brush
- scribing block
- metal saw
- wood saw, fine
- screw tap, size M4 or M5
- center punch
- hammer
- awl
- diamond file

THE MATERIALS

For knifemaking you have a wide variety of materials for blade and handle at your hands. Especially with respect to steel types, it is difficult to keep an overview and to decide on a steel. We will try to bring some order to this chaos.

3.1 The Blade Steels

The market is filled with blade steels which compete for attention among knifemakers. The decision on the right steel is a science in itself.

In principle, decisive for the choice of steel is its later use. In other words, which kind of blade should be created from the steel and what is it supposed to do? For a Bowie knife with a 10" blade there are different requirements than for a scalpel. With respect to our hidden tang knife, we first have to decide whether the blade should be stainless or not.

It has to be said that truly rust-resisting quality is only achieved with the types of stainless steel which can't be hardened, and blade steels are hardened. Though with a chromium content of 13 percent and higher, the expression "stainless" is used—nevertheless steel can rust under adverse conditions.

The blade steels on offer can roughly be divided into five categories:

- low-alloy carbon steels
- high-alloy stainless steels
- high-alloy tool steels (which can rust)
- powder metallurgical steels
- Damascus steels

Low-alloy carbon steels like C60, O-1, or 52100 don't possess many other components besides carbon (between 0.4 and 1.5 percent). Carbon is the decisive element in the steel: It allows the steel to be hardened.

During the hardening process (heating, then rapidly cooling down the steel), a structural change in the material takes place. The treated material is under tension, which contributes to its resistance. Besides that, carbides are formed in the process— tiny carbon compounds which are extremely hard and almost indestructible.

In industry carbon steels are used as springs, for example. These steel types are not stainless, but have their advantages nevertheless: They have a fine molecular structure and can be used for equally fine and sharp blade edges. In addition, knife blades of carbon steels can be sharpened easily and overall have a high elasticity. There is a reason that many bladesmiths still prefer the "good, old" carbon steel.

A difficult choice: The selection of knife steels on offer is huge. In the image you can see Japanese suminagashi steel (top) with 22 layers and material with three layers.
Photo: Dick – Feine Werkzeuge

Most knife blades are composed of stainless, high-alloy steel types like 440C, ATS-34, AUS-8, or 1.4112. These steels contain at least 13 percent chromium, which is the reason for their resistance to rust. In addition, the steel contains carbon—usually between 0.4 and 1.5 percent—and various other elements such as vanadium or molybdenum, and sometimes also tungsten, cobalt, nitrogen, or niobium.

The rust-resisting property in principle has to be traded against a somewhat reduced elasticity. Furthermore, the structure (and the blade edge) isn't as fine because the additional components of the alloy tend to form bigger carbides. Blades of stainless steel tend to take more effort to sharpen.

High-alloy tool steels like D2, M2, or A2 possess an exotic status among the blade steels since they are high-alloy but not stainless due to a chromium content below 13 percent. These steel types are usually optimized with respect to their mechanical quality, which makes them interesting for blade steels. Their edge-holding property is very high (which means the blade stays sharp for a longer period of time during use) while their resistance to bending loads is also good.

Powder metallurgically (PM) manufactured steel types like RWL-34, CPM-S30V, or M390 have set out to conquer the knife world in the last ten years. These steels are not melted in a usual way. Instead, the fluid steel is sprayed to create a fine powder which is then "baked" into solid steel under high pressure and temperature. PM steels can contain higher percentages of other elements than conventional steel (which can only take in about 1.5 percent of carbon). Besides that, its structure is finer and more homogenous (the carbides are smaller and distributed more evenly) than that of conventional steel. This combination of qualities turns these modern high-end blade steels into all-round talents.

Damascus steel consists of many layers made out of two or more different types of steel which are welded together in the forging fire. Originally, this procedure—which is several thousand years old—was developed to combine the qualities of different steels (hardness and elasticity) in a single piece of work. Even today, Damascus blades are surrounded by mythical reports which claim they have mystical abilities.

Today, Damascus blades are mainly used because of the fascinating patterns that can be created. The typical structure is created by etching: During this process, the different types of steel are corroded by the etching medium (acid) to a different degree, which leads to a different color and a relief-like pattern after applying the acid for a longer period of time. The patterns in the steel are created by etching and polishing thereafter, but also by twisting the steel and other procedures. For mosaic

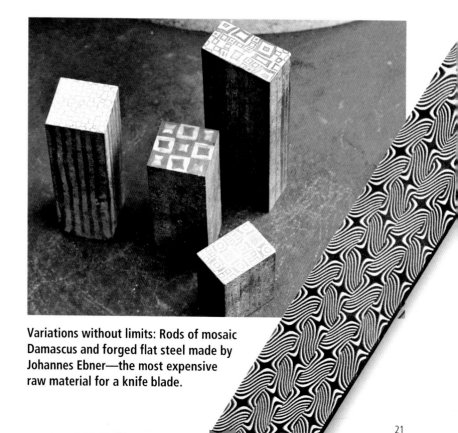

Variations without limits: Rods of mosaic Damascus and forged flat steel made by Johannes Ebner—the most expensive raw material for a knife blade.

Damascus, the material is put together from a multitude of parts. There are hardly any limits with respect to the variety of patterns and to combining materials. Meanwhile, even Damascus steels are available as stainless materials.

A special case is the powder metallurgically manufactured Damascus steel from the Swedish company Damasteel. Powder of different types of steel (RWL-34 and PMC-27) is stacked, then sintered. This stainless material is available with various patterns and is easy to work with.

A special case is also represented by the so-called sandwich steels, which are composed of several steel layers. Usually this means that a hard central layer (for the edge) is framed by softer outer layers which provide elasticity and are often resistant to rust. This kind of construction is especially common in Japan. Often "blue paper steel" (Aogami)—a very pure, tungsten-alloy carbon steel made by Hitachi—is used for the core.

Which steel you decide on is, above all, also a question of taste and price. For your very first handmade knife you'll hardly use mosaic Damascus, which has a price of nearly $700. For a start, rather cheap carbon steels or stainless steels like 440C or N690 are quite inviting. With them, you can't go wrong. And if something bad happens during work and you ruin your work piece, then you haven't lost a huge amount of money.

During this workshop we worked exclusively with Damasteel Damascus, which is Heinrich Schmidbauer's preferred material. Because of this, we also describe the process of etching in this volume. What we didn't do ourselves was the hardening and annealing. Correct heat treatment for modern steels requires a certain technical effort. Without a special oven with control over the exact temperature curve, hardening is almost impossible.

Because of this, we outsourced this important step to a professional company. The suppliers of blade steel and knifemaking

tools (see suppliers in the appendix) can help you with this and name appropriate companies for hardening.

WHICH ELEMENT IS GOOD FOR WHAT?

Here are the most important alloy elements for steel and their effects

Carbon (C)
Raises the steel's hardness and resistance to wear; it needs to be present for the development of carbides. It is the most important element of any alloy.

Chromium (Cr)
Forms hard carbides (high resistance to wear and abrasion), provides resistance to corrosion, is important for thorough hardening, and provides good tempering properties.

Nickel (Ni)
Is positive for toughness; it doesn't form carbides but only mixed crystals. Provides protection against corrosion in combination with chromium.

Molybdenum (Mo)
Properties similar to chromium, but more intense. Combination with chromium results in hardness at elevated temperatures. Molybdenum also forms special, very stable carbides.

Tungsten (W)
Forms very hard, stress-resistant carbides; in steel it provides hardness at elevated temperatures; can replace molybdenum up to a certain degree; and it increases thermal conductivity (important for hardening).

Phosphorus (P)
Not wanted because it makes steel brittle.

Vanadium (V)
Makes crystals finer (a finer molecular structure) and, like tungsten, forms hard, wear-resistant carbides which provide high edge-holding quality.

Titanium (Ti)
Forms the hardest of all metal carbides (almost reaches the hardness of diamond) and thus provides a big boost to edge holding.

Manganese (Mn)
Simplifies casting, forging, and rolling the steel and enhances the steel with thorough hardening and viscosity.

Cobalt (Co)
Doesn't form carbides but only mixed crystals, enhances hardness at elevated temperatures, and inhibits crystal growth (fine structure).

Silicon (Si)
Has a favorable influence on elasticity (is part of spring steel alloys because of this).

Nitrogen (N)
Enhances the corrosion resistance of steels.

Sulphur (S)
Like phosphorus, it isn't wanted, but small amounts are added to so-called machine steel to make it easier to cut the steel..

3.2 Handle Materials

For a hidden tang knife, in general, only natural handle materials fit best. An important consideration with respect to bone and horn materials is a sufficient density within the piece. Here, the tang must fit very tightly. The classic star is stag horn, but the available selection covers everything from antelope horn to prohibitively expensive narwhal tusk to oosik—fossilized walrus penis bone. Some materials (e.g. elephant tusk or tortoiseshell) are illegal to use. In these cases you need a CITES certificate from the vendor. Without such a statement of origin for the material you are likely to get into a great deal of trouble!

Add to this list a huge variety of woods, everything from wood from native fruit trees to African ebony and American desert ironwood. A very practical material is stabilized wood, which has been treated with epoxy and is thus waterproof and durable. Also, these stabilized materials don't shrink, unlike untreated woods. The same treatment is also used on bone. Stabilized giraffe bone (from the shin), for example, is a beautiful, dense material with a smooth surface.

Handle materials without cracks: Stabilized woods are made durable with epoxy. A wide variety of colors are also available.

Photo: www.novacula.de

A typical Scandinavian variant is a handle made of stacked leather rings. They are placed on the tang and pressed together with a screw or rivet at the handle butt. The rings for this kind of construction can be punched out of strong leather. The whole handle is ground into shape only after assembly.

A very distinguished look is a combination of different handle materials. Thus you can bring together horn, bone, wood, and leather on a single knife, separated only by thin layers of vulcanized fiber or nickel silver. The latter is a favorite material for the mountings on the handle i.e. a guard or ferrule on the front and butt or end cap at the rear. As an alternative, brass is often used, but you can also consider aluminum, titanium, or stainless steel. Here you can let your creativity run free. But you shouldn't forget that the handle is in contact with your hand. Thus you should avoid metals that rust or discolor.

Examples of beautiful combinations of handle materials by the companies Helle (Norway) and Herbertz (Germany):

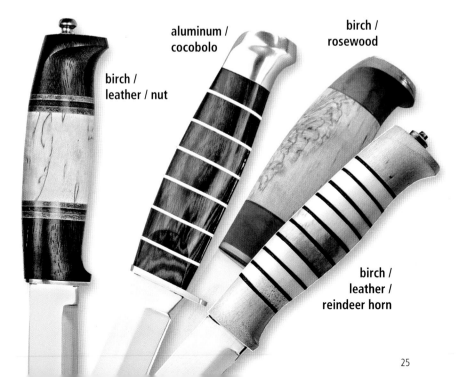

birch /
leather / nut

aluminum /
cocobolo

birch /
rosewood

birch /
leather /
reindeer horn

THE BLADE

The basic material for our blade is a piece of flat steel that is 0.118" (3 mm) thick. From this, we first cut off a piece with the right length. It is important that we count at least two thirds of the blade length for the tang so it reaches far enough into the handle later on for a stable connection. Our blade should become rather short so we cut off a piece that is 7" (18 cm). Of this, 3.93" (10 cm) are counted for the blade, 3.14" (8 cm) for the tang.

The correct length: At least two thirds of the total blade length should be counted for the tang so it reaches far enough into the handle.

Marking with a waterproof pen: Our work piece will have a length of 7" (18 cm), about three are planned for the tang.

Protecting your work: Place pieces of felt between the blade steel and the vise jaws to avoid damage.

Sawing off: With the metal saw, cut the blade steel along the marked line. If available, a band saw works faster.

Transition: Draw a line where the blade and the handle meet. The length of the blade is thus defined.

Now we draw the shape of the blade plus the tang onto the material with a waterproof felt pen.

You can also make a drawing on paper first and then transfer it onto a cardboard template which serves as an aid for drawing on the steel. The curves, however, shouldn't be drawn freehand, but with the aid of a curve tool. This can be a professional French curve template or any object with a fitting curve and a good edge, like a cup or a plate. The tang should be slightly tapered so the handle fits on tightly later on.

Auxiliary device: To draw the curves, use anything with an appropriate curve and a proper edge.

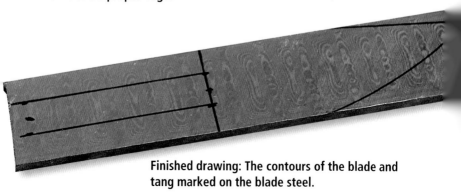

Finished drawing: The contours of the blade and tang marked on the blade steel.

To cut the blade to size, we first drill a row of small holes (0.078" [2.0 mm]) along the drawn line with a drill press. Clamp the steel blank into the vise.

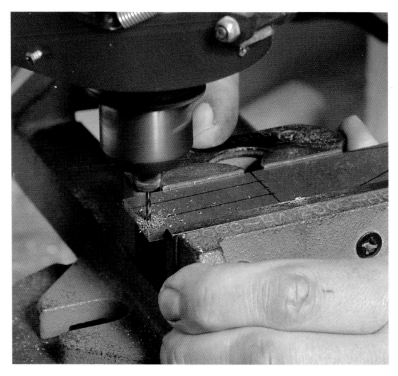

Pre-drilling: Drill holes with a 0.078" (2.0 mm) drill bit at close intervals along the outside of the marked line.

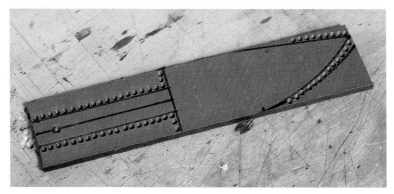

Pattern of holes: This is what the blade steel should look like after the holes have been drilled all around.

After the piece has been drilled, clamp it into the normal vise and cut the shape out with the metal saw. Use a band saw to complete this step even faster.

Sawing the shape: Use the metal saw to saw through the drill holes and form the edges of the blade.

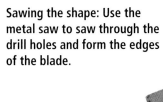

Coarse contour: After sawing, the shape of the blade is more or less complete. Refining the shape is next.

To smooth the contours of the blade, we work along the edges with a coarse metal file. In doing so, file down to the marked line. For the last tenth a finer file should be used to avoid taking too much of the material off.

Filing the edges: With a coarse metal file, smooth the contours of the blade. Leave a fraction of material outside the marked line.

Exact shaping: With a finer file, remove the remaining material until the desired shape is reached.

Intermediate step:
The blade contour is complete;
the tang is still waiting to be filed.

As before: The tang is also smoothed with the coarse file first followed by the finer file.

Almost invisible: The tang should be slightly conical to guarantee a tight fit in the handle without any play.

/CTP

Now it's time for the difficult step, shaping the wedge of the blade. First, grind the blade flat; a hollow grind can't be done with the file. Now mark the ricasso on both sides of the blade. The transition between the wedged area and the flat ricasso can be straight or oblique (which in general looks better). To mark the blade edge exactly in the center, use a scribing block. As an alternative, you can scribe from both sides. Then you can see possible deviations.

A question of aesthetics: Draw the transition between the wedged area to the flat ricasso obliquely on both sides (it can also be straight).

Prior to scribing, you can paint the small area with quick-drying, dark blue layout dye. The needle of the scriber leaves a clearly visible, tidy line in this dye.

Precious aid: Prior to scribing the blade edge, apply layout dye to the area.

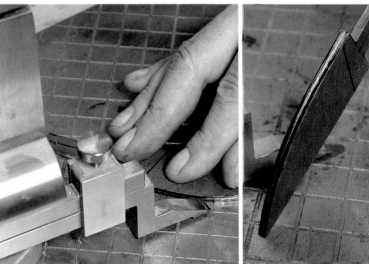

Precise work: Scribe the exact center of the blade edge with a professional scribing block. The line is clearly visible in the blue layout dye.

Now we start shaping the blade. Clamp the knife into the vise at its tang and begin to shape the wedge with the file. For this we start 0.078" (2 mm) away from the ricasso and work from the lower edge (the blade edge) towards the back of the blade. Directly at the ricasso, do not file up to the blade's back or beyond or you may not be able to achieve a good transition later on. After we have worked along the entire blade length evenly, use a finer file to remove the coarse file marks left behind. Also, refine the line along the ricasso with the finer file.

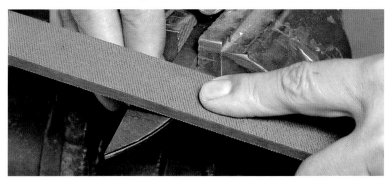

Starting point: Begin to shape the wedge a bit in front of the drawn ricasso.

First traces: The filed wedge starts immediately in front of the drawn line.

After we have worked along the entire blade length evenly, use a finer file to remove the coarse file marks left behind. Also, refine the line along the ricasso with the finer file.

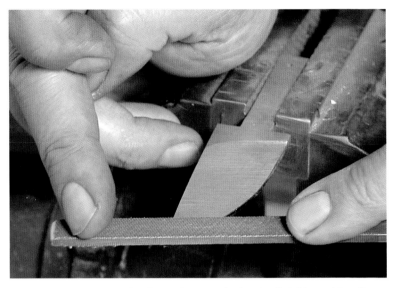

Evenness is the thing: Slowly work towards the tip, finishing with a finer file.

Critical point: The transition between the ricasso to the back of the blade is filed obliquely.

Final touches: The transition between the ricasso and the filed part of the blade should be round. To achieve this, carefully remove the material.

In the end, the transition from the ricasso to the filed area (up at the blade's back) is rounded. For this, you carefully take off material in the direction of filing to achieve a smooth transition. This is the most difficult part of the whole procedure. You need a sensitive hand for this. Afterwards, the blade is turned around and the whole procedure is repeated on the other side. On the latter edge leave about 0.039" (1 mm) of material. Only after hardening is the edge filed and sharpened.

Working with the file is strenuous and also requires a certain amount of experience. For beginners, we recommend practicing with a cheap work piece to get a feel for the file and how to achieve level surfaces before filing an expensive steel. One pitfall to avoid is inadvertently tilting the file to and fro—the resulting surface is not flat, but rounded.

You can save yourself time and energy if you use a belt sander. But this is a big investment which requires a certain amount of space in your workshop. Working on a belt sander also requires a lot of skill, and because it is a power tool there are certain safety concerns to consider. In any case, we recommend that you don't start out working with a belt sander, but start working with files to achieve a feeling for the work. Many knifemakers stick to the file in the long run to construct authentic "handmade" knives.

Filing is followed by touching up the blade with abrasive cloth or sandpaper. Tear off a strip of sandpaper about 0.393" (10 mm) wide, wrap it around a file, and start sanding lengthwise. Start with grit P180 and work up towards grit P800 in several steps. In doing so, only change to the next finer grit when the surface of the blade seems to be perfect.

With each progressive step, change the direction of sanding. For example, move across the blade with grit P240, lengthwise with P400, across with P600, and finally lengthwise with grit P800. With this kind of finishing, the marks of the previous round of sanding are removed most effectively. Working strenuously with the sandpaper is decisive for the quality of the blade. Here you shouldn't stop too early.

Our blade is now ready for hardening. We leave the heat treatment to a specialized company and continue afterwards.

Precise work: To precisely grind the blade, wrap a piece of abrasive cloth around a file. Use a piece of wood as a base for the blade so the sandpaper doesn't get caught on the tip.

Strenuous: Polish the blade manually with ascending grit numbers and sand the blade at right angles—sand across the width of the blade then down the length of the blade (the final polish should always be lengthwise).

A little trick: When the blade is clamped in a way that the tip vanishes, you can file along the back without any problem.

Neat finish: The back of the blade is also worked with ever smoother abrasive cloth and sandpaper (up to grit P800).

Done for now:
The blade is now ready for hardening and etching. A threaded rod will be added later on.

ETCHING AND FINISHING THE BLADE

Our blade made of stainless Damasteel Damascus was hardened for us to 59 degrees of Rockwell C. When the blade returns from hardening, we first check whether warping has occurred. Sometimes a blade can warp during heat treatment. Luckily, with Damasteel warping rarely occurs and our blade came back straight as an arrow. Bent blades have to be cautiously straightened prior to further work.

To make the pretty wave pattern of our Damascus visible, the blade has to be etched. For this, it has to be exposed to acid which corrodes the softer parts of the steel more than the harder ones. This carves the pattern out on the surface.

Starting point: Our Damasteel blade comes back from hardening looking like this. The Damascus pattern is still almost invisible.

Supplies for etching: Water boiler, plastic bucket, glass receptacle, and 37% sulphuric acid (accumulator acid). Everything has to be labeled carefully!

We use sulphuric acid of 37 percent. You can also use ferric chloride ($FeCl_3$), which is less aggressive. Therefore the etching times are longer and the process can be more easily controlled. With fresh sulphuric acid, most times two minutes are sufficient; with ferric chloride, the necessary time varies between 5 and 45 minutes, depending on the type of steel and the desired depth of etching. In general, sulphuric acid is used for powder-metallurgical steel like Damasteel, ferric chloride is used for carbon steels.

Put about 1 to 2 cups (0.25 to 0.5 liters) of sulphuric acid in a proper glass receptacle and cautiously heat it in a warm bath of water to about 122°F (50°C). The acid "works" better in a warm state. The amount of acid depends on the size of the glass. Using a funnel and rubber gloves, put the acid back into the bottle after use.

Preparing the water bath: Pour the heated water into the bucket.

Pour the acid into the glass receptacle. In our case the acid was already used a couple of times before, which is revealed by its color.

Heating: The glass receptacle is put into the bath of water to heat the acid up to about 122°F (50°C).

Caution: The etching has to be done outdoors because the acid really does produce "etching" fumes which under no circumstances should be inhaled! Even in a well-ventilated room the fumes are a dangerous threat to your health!

The heated acid may fume slightly, but it should not boil. When it has reached the right temperature, cautiously put the blade into the acid. In doing so, you have to be careful to avoid splashing. Since you need to avoid any direct skin contact with the acid, it is recommended that you use tongs. Additionally, perhaps you can attach a wire to the blade, or hold it with a magnet.

The amount of time needed for etching depends on the desired depth of the etching, the steel used, and on the state and temperature of the acid. During etching, take the blade out of the fluid every now and then and check the status. If you leave the blade in the acidic bath for too long, the steel will corrode too much and start to "fringe" along the borders, especially in the area of the edge, where the material only has a thickness of 0.019" up to 0.039" (0.5 to 1.0 mm).

Submerging: Carefully submerge the blade in the acid without splashing. The acid may fume a little, but it shouldn't boil. If the acid produces foam, the heat has to be reduced.

How strongly you etch the blade is not least a question of personal taste. When the desired depth of etching has been reached, thoroughly rinse the blade in water and let it dry. The blade now displays an even gray hue in which the pattern of the steel is clearly visible.

Check:
Take the blade out of the acid several times to check its status.

Rinsing:
After rinsing the knife with clear water, the etched pattern is visible. The longer the blade stays in the acid, the deeper the etching. If you miss the right length of time, the blade may "fringe" along its borders and the surface will be damaged.

Gray in gray: Prior to finishing, the surface displays a uniformly gray color; only finishing will reveal the pretty contrast.

Now the finishing begins: Grind the surface of the blade with sandpaper with grit from P800 to P1200. To help with polishing, use a square piece of wood wrapped in a strip of sandpaper. The wood block provides a level surface and prevents injuries. If you file freehand without an aid, you risk poking the blade tip through the abrasive paper directly into your finger.

By sanding, the upper, harder part of the blade structure, which was corroded less by etching, is smoothed and polished. The deeper-lying and softer layers, in comparison, keep their darker color. Thus the Damascus pattern is carved out. If you only achieved a shallow etching, you have to be careful when finishing, for otherwise it is easy to sand away the pretty pattern rather quickly.

Finishing: The upper (hard) layer is polished to a shine with sandpaper wrapped around a wood block.

Across: Polish the tang and ricasso without removing material from the critical transition to the area that has already been ground!

Our old trick: In order to work on the back, clamp the blade in such a way that the tip vanishes between the jaws of the vise.

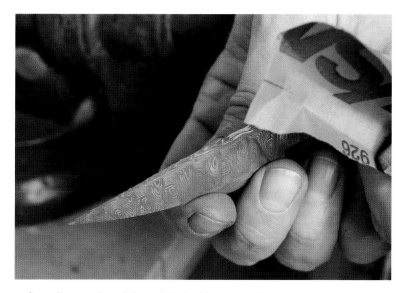

Refine all around: Lightly polish the blade's back, too, in order to make the Damascus pattern visible.

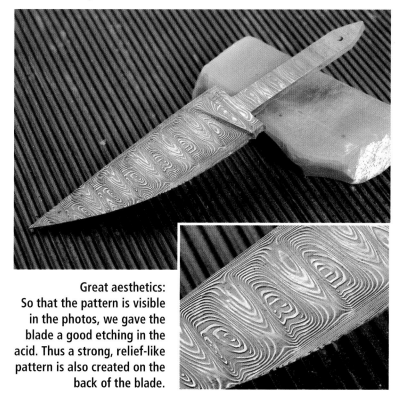

Great aesthetics: So that the pattern is visible in the photos, we gave the blade a good etching in the acid. Thus a strong, relief-like pattern is also created on the back of the blade.

Now our blade lacks only one thing: sharpness. We left about 0.039" (1 mm) of material around the area where the blade's edge will later form. Now we work the material with a diamond file. But prior to that, we wrap a few layers of adhesive tape around the tang for a better grip. Of course you can always construct and mount the handle before sharpening the blade. This actually reduces the risk of injuries while working on the blade. If you sharpen the edge first, later you will have to cover the blade with adhesive tape to avoid slipping into the sharp edge.

With a bit of training, sharpening with the diamond file can be done freehand. Align the file at an angle between 15 and 30 degrees to the blade and draw it evenly across the edge. Grind both sides up to 0.0 mm; change to the other side when you are able to feel a burr on the first side.

Ready for the final polish: After the pretty etching pattern has been revealed, wrap adhesive tape around the tang for a better grip.

The blade angle depends on how the knife will be used and the skills of its user. The shallower the angle, the sharper the edge. But the blade becomes more sensitive with an ever smaller angle. If you want to be on the safe side, choose a slightly larger angle; if you want the knife to be sharper, make it smaller. But whichever angle you choose, it is always important to make the angle constant. If you are not confident, you can also use sharpening devices which provide a constant angle. But it is more fun to do it manually.

Done freehand: The blade edge is sharpened evenly on both sides with a diamond file.

Tip: you can simply turn the blade around, since the file works in both directions.

Thereafter the edge is stropped with a fine natural stone. It smooths the edge and provides a fine sharpness. A final buffing at the polishing wheel makes the whole thing perfect. But be cautious: stropping the edge at the polishing wheel (for this we clamped a drill into a support) is potentially dangerous! As long as the rotation is pointing away from the edge, there is no danger. But if you are not careful and the wheel rotates against the edge, there is a great risk that the edge will get caught and dragged along in an uncontrollable way.

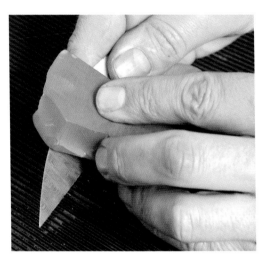

Fine sharpness: To give the edge its final smoothness, it is stropped with a fine natural stone.

Polish: Buffing at the polishing wheel brings an even finer surface to the edge and maximizes sharpness and cutting abilities.

Be careful: The polishing wheel should never rotate towards the edge, as the edge might get caught and cause serious injuries!

Now that our blade is ground completely, hardened, etched, finished, and sharpened, the handle can be mounted.

Our work in an intermediate state: The blade of the hidden tang knife is completely finished. Now it is time to attach the handle.

THE HANDLE

Mounting handle scales on the left and right of a knife with full tang is relatively easy. To connect a single-piece handle in a tightly fitting and durable way with a hidden tang knife requires some more effort and skills.

The simple solution with respect to a hidden tang is that the handle—after fitting the drill hole inside to the tang—is simply glued onto the tang. When executed professionally, this construction holds without any problems. To be on the safe side, you can secure the connection further by means of a rivet or threaded joint. The latter is the solution which takes the most effort and the one we decided to use.

Start by welding a threaded rod of stainless steel (thread size M4) onto the tang. In theory you could also cut the threads

Preparations: From a long, threaded rod (M4 thread size in our case; for bigger knives M5 is also suitable) cut off an appropriate piece.

Lengthening: Weld the threaded rod to the tang. Later on it will provide a stable, screwed connection with the handle.

directly on the tang (if it is long enough), but this is anything but easy, since our tang is rectangular in shape. If you don't have a welding machine or don't have the means to weld stainless steel, you can give the job to a professional for a small fee. It is important to leave as much of the tang as possible in order to achieve maximum stability for the knife.

We use oosik for the handle material and stainless Damasteel Damascus for the front element and the pommel. The choice of material doesn't have any influence on the steps described in the following passages. Nevertheless, the thickness of the material for the pommel shouldn't be too thin because we need to fit a blind hole with thread there later on. The minimum should be 0.157" (4 mm).

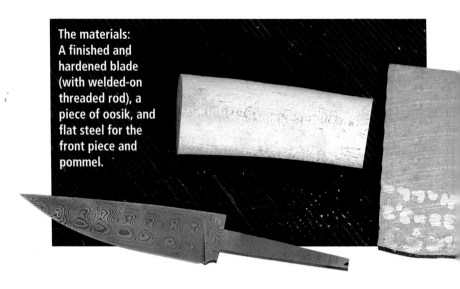

The materials: A finished and hardened blade (with welded-on threaded rod), a piece of oosik, and flat steel for the front piece and pommel.

The lengths of the front end and the pommel are estimated generously and two appropriate pieces are cut out of the flat material. On the front element, we mark the width of the tang centrally and drill the elongated hole for holding it. Our blade has a thickness of 0.125" (3.2 mm). Thus we pick up a 0.098" (2.5 mm) drill bit and set a row of holes next to each other. Thus you don't have to use the milling machine. Afterwards, the elongated hole is worked on and smoothed with a small, flat file.

Place the front piece onto the tang every now and then to check the fit. Only by doing this can you guarantee a clean fit without gaps. Be cautious: just a few movements with the file can make a decisive difference!

Now we look to the handle piece. First it is cut to the desired length and perhaps filed to shape coarsely. Then mark the hole for drilling. It doesn't necessarily have to be centered. If you place the handle next to the blade the way it is supposed to be located later on, you can draw the position of the tang on the side of the handle piece, then transfer the markings to the front end.

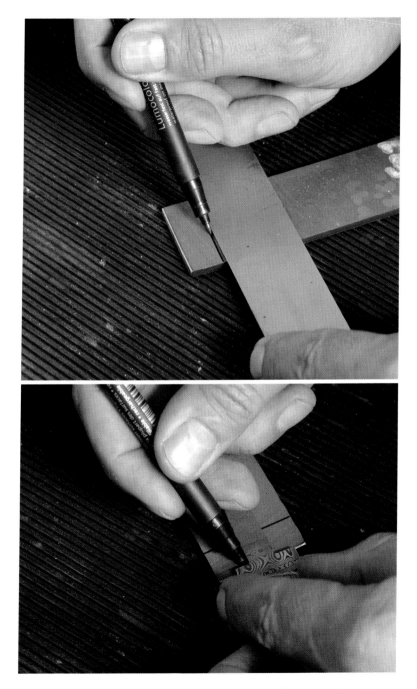

Marking: Mark a strip for the front element on the flat material and draw the width of the tang as a measurement for the elongated hole.

Sawing: Cut the marked pieces for the front element and the pommel (see page 67) from the flat steel.

The handle piece is ready to be chucked and the hole can be drilled. For this you need a drill press. The diameter of the drill hole should be small enough to leave some play to adjust the hole to the tang later on. We suggest using a 0.157" (4.0 mm) drill bit. The hole is widened a bit at the front end by means of a small saw blade so that the tang fits inside as exactly as possible. Here you will need to frequently check the fit, too.

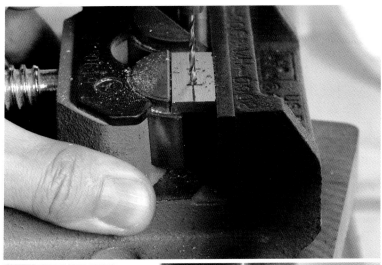

Drilling the elongated hole: The center of the piece is marked, then drill holes are set in a row next to each other.

Improvising: First set the holes next to each other, then drill through. Thus you avoid using a milling machine—a tool that is not too common in the workshop.

Refinement: The elongated hole is smoothed and adjusted to the tang by means of a small file, resulting in a neat fit without any gaps.

Now the handle is filed to its final shape, if necessary, and smoothed with abrasive cloth. Then we continue with the front element. The outer contour of the handle (the front end) is marked on the element; then we shape it accordingly with a file. Towards the end of this work, it is recommended that you regularly compare it with the handle piece to avoid taking off too much material.

A good sense of distance is needed: Place the handle piece on the finished blade at the same position it will hold later on. Then mark the position of the tang on the handle piece.

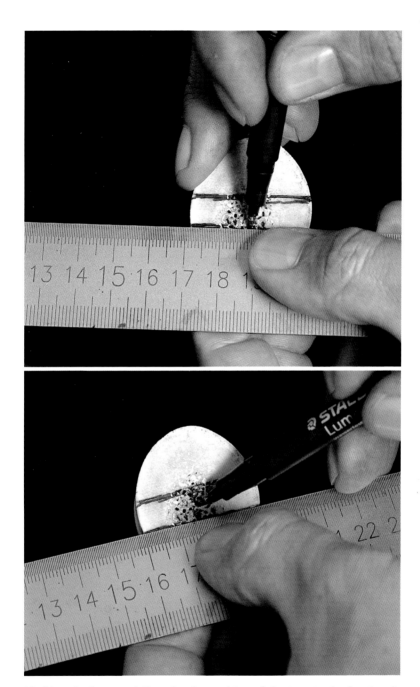

Marking the front end: Transfer the position of the tang to the front end of the handle piece, which is already cut to length. Then determine the center and mark the drill hole.

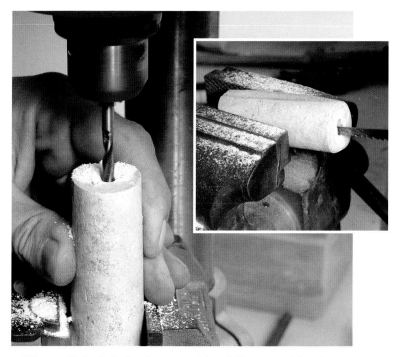

Drilling: Drill the hole for the tang with a drill press. Widen the hole at the front end of the handle slightly with a saw.

Precise work: The widened hole has to be adjusted to the tang's contour to assure a perfect fit. Regularly check the fit of the tang with the front element and the pommel.

Working the handle: Shape the handle to the desired contour with wood rasp and file. During your work, don't forget to take the position of the drill hole into account!

Finished for now: Our oosik handle already has the right shape; it is slightly curved and conical towards the end.

Now we continue working on the pommel. It will hold the knife and its handle together later on. For this we have to set a blind hole (drill as deeply as possible to reach a maximum thread depth, but don't drill through the whole piece!) The position of the hole must fit the location of the drill hole in the handle. It may be centered exactly, but it doesn't have to be. The diameter of the hole and the thread which we now cut into it has, of course, to correspond to the threaded rod, which we welded to the tang.

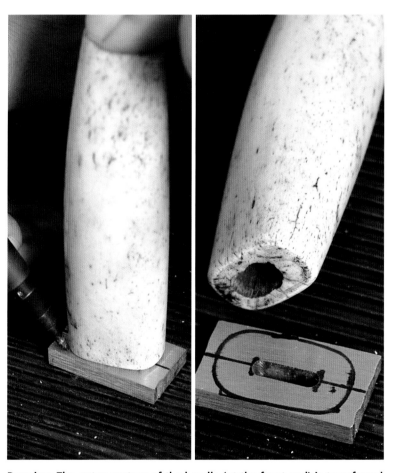

Drawing: The outer contour of the handle (at the front end) is transferred onto the front element. Hitting exactly the right position is easiest with a pushed-through tang (different from the photo).

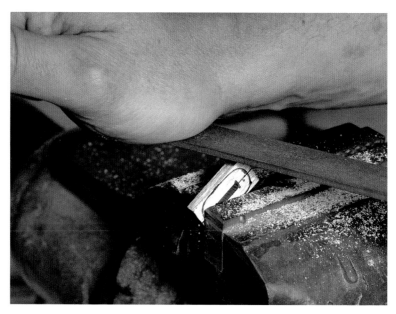

Shaping the contour: Shape the outer contour of the front element with the file to align it with the marked line.

Extra: We enhance our front element with some decorative filework all-around the side facing the handle.

Ready for mounting: Put the front element aside for a while as we look to the pommel next.

Drilling a blind hole: Center-punch and drill the piece with a 0.125" (3.2 mm) bit, corresponding to the threaded rod. (Depending on the handle, the hole can also be located off to one side.)

Tapping: Tap a thread into the blind hole (not drilled through completely), which corresponds in size to the threaded rod on the tang (in our case M4).

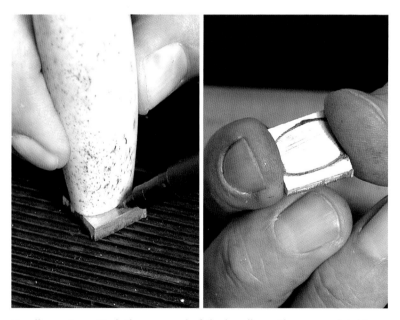

Handle contour: Mark the rear end of the handle on the pommel, taking into account the position of the drill holes in the pommel and the handle.

Shaping the pommel: Like the front element earlier, now the pommel is fitted to the rear of the handle.

Ready for the final steps: Handle piece (center), front element (right), and pommel (left; with a slight conical shape) are ready for mounting.

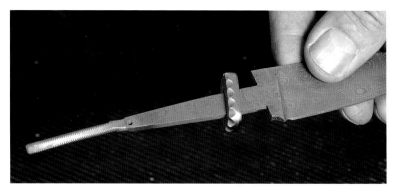

Testing the fit: To adjust the length of the threaded rod, first the front element, then the handle are placed on the tang.

Too much is better than too little: The threaded rod must protrude far enough for the pommel to be screwed on.

Now comes the most difficult part, or at least the most strenuous part, of the whole enterprise. The length of the threaded rod has to be exact so that the pommel, when screwed on tightly, sits in exactly the right position and is flush with the handle. This means filing, assembling the parts, screwing on the pommel, checking the position, disassembling the parts again, filing, assembling, screwing on the pommel, and so on…

Important: when the correct length is achieved, the threaded rod has to be deburred, otherwise the thread will "eat itself up" later on. Stainless steel is thus very critical.

Test: When the pommel is screwed on tightly, it should not sit at an angle as depicted here, but should fit in a way that it is flush with the contours of the handle all the way around.

Strenuous: The threaded rod is shortened to the exact length with a file. Check the fit every now and then as you file. Upon completion, the thread is deburred.

When all the parts fit together, the outer surfaces of the handle, front piece, and pommel are sanded with abrasive paper. Start with grit P180, then continue in steps up to grit P600. You should take your time with this work, because only then can you achieve perfect quality.

Finishing: Step by step, the handle is given a proper surface quality with abrasive cloth. This requires a lot of time, but it is worth the effort.

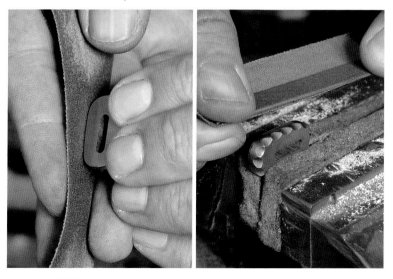

Up to grit P600: The outsides of the front element and pommel are polished in several steps, starting with grit P180 and ending with P600.

At last, now you can start the final assembly. For this, the smaller drill hole at the rear part of the handle piece is closed with a piece of easy-to-remove protective tape, and the handle piece is clamped in the vise with the bigger drill hole showing upwards. Mix a proper amount of epoxy. Then everything has to happen quickly before the adhesive hardens. Fill the drill hole inside the handle. The adhesive should fill up the entire space without bubbles.

Then the front element is put on the tang and the tang is put into the handle. Glue which runs out has to be wiped off immediately! Then we turn the handle around, pull off the tape and screw on the pommel. The position of the pommel has to be perfect before the glue starts to dry, otherwise you'll have a rather big problem at hand.

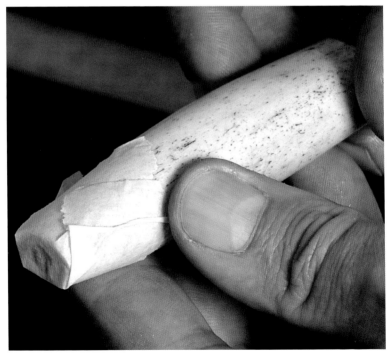

Closing the hole: Tape the smaller hole at the rear end of the handle piece shut in order to fill in the epoxy glue. The other parts should be placed close at hand.

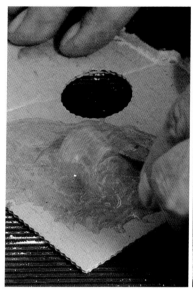

Everything has to happen quickly: Prepare the two-component epoxy glue and fill the handle piece with it.

A little trick: To prevent bubbles from forming in the adhesive within the handle, poke around inside the drill hole with a thin rod or awl before all the epoxy has been filled into the hole.

Small amounts of glue excess can be removed from the corners with a pointed object while the glue is still partially liquid. As a final step clean the whole knife with glue remover from the home improvement store.

That's it. Our hidden tang knife is finished. Now we move on to the sheath.

In a jiffy: The handle piece (together with the front element) is placed on the tang, the tape is removed, the pommel screwed on, and spilled glue is wiped off.

Final steps: Screw the pommel on tightly (protective leather in the vise is the best way). Remove partially liquid glue from the corners.

Finished: Clean the knife all around with solvent to remove any excess glue. That's it!

THE SHEATH

There are many ways to provide a home for the fixed blade knife. Besides the different types of sheaths (open or closed sheaths, sheaths with metal tips, or quiver-like sheaths) and materials (leather, kydex, cordura), there are many variants with respect to how they are made. For our classic fixed blade knife with Nordic design, we decided upon a traditional quiver-like sheath made from leather.

The design is courtesy of Heinrich Schmidbauer, who doesn't provide the sheath with an ordinary seam, but with a 0.118" (3 mm) wide leather strap that is braided around the edge of the sheath.

Raw material: A sheet of strong orthopedic leather.

TOOLS LIST

- split leather (orthopedic leather)
- soda
- leather dye
- ~5 feet (1.5 m) leather strap, 0.118" (3 mm) wide
- pencil (blunt) or pen
- abrasive cloth, grit P180
- superglue
- adjustable groover
- drill bit 0.078" (2.0 mm)
- drilling press
- carpenter's knife or shoemaker's knife
- brush for leather dye
- harness needle
- clamps for fixing

Drawing: The knife's length is generously drawn on the leather.

The most important thing to remember when making a sheath, of course, is safety. The sheath, under all circumstances, has to prevent the blade from piercing through and it has to hold the knife permanently. Our raw material is split leather, also called orthopedic leather. From a large sheet of leather, we first cut off an appropriate piece for our sheath. It has about the same length as the knife and three times its width—plus an additional couple of centimeters to be on the safe side. If in doubt, it's better to cut off a piece that is too large.

Cutting to size:
The piece is
approximately three
times as wide as the knife.

Place the leather in lukewarm water, in which we first dissolve two tablespoons of soda. After drying, the soda provides sufficient stiffness and thus stability to the sheath. Besides that, it gives the leather a darker color. In general, the more soda is dissolved in water, the darker and harder the leather becomes later on. The leather ought to be in the water for at least ten to fifteen minutes so it can absorb the water fully and evenly. After that, the soaked leather is put on an absorbent cloth and dried from both sides with light pressure. It takes hours or even days until the leather is completely dry again.

Panacea: Place the leather into lukewarm water, in which two tablespoonfuls of soda have been dissolved, for 10 to 15 minutes. The soda makes the leather stiff later on.

Trick: Mid-way through the time the leather sits in the water, knead the leather so the moisture is evenly absorbed.

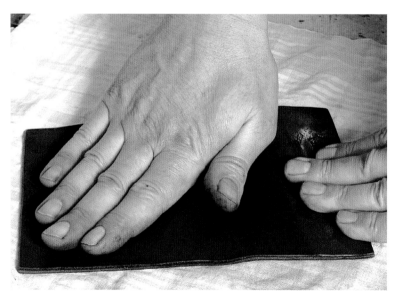

Preparing: Place the leather on an absorbent cloth and dry it with slight pressure.

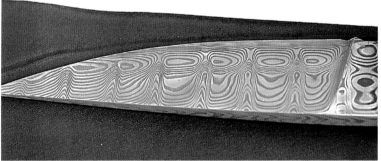

Sketching: Then, starting at the cutting edge side, draw the contour of the knife onto the leather, adding a few millimeters to the dimensions.

Thereafter place the knife onto the piece of leather at the edge with the blade pointing outwards. Draw the contour with a pen, then cut out the shape with a carpenter's knife or shoemaker's knife. Fold the leather across the knife, then draw the contour on the other side and cut it out as well (the photos provide a better explanation of how this is done). It is important that enough material is left for the seam allowance.

Drawing aid: if you don't have a French curve template, you can also use other appropriate things as a guide for cutting.

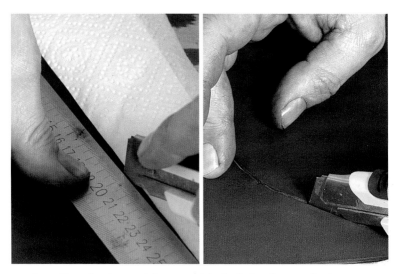

Cutting off: Make the straight cuts with the help of a metal ruler. Cutting a curve by freehand is extremely difficult.

To achieve a clean cut, a ruler (a French curve template), or, as a replacement, a batten, plate, or something similar should be used. In general, be careful with moist leather! It is recommended that you cut your fingernails prior to working with the leather because ugly prints will be permanently visible on the leather!

Current status: The first curve is cut, but the shape is still not clear.

Folding: After one side has been cut, fold the leather over the knife's back.

Mirror image: Draw the opposite side (with a sufficient add-on for the seam allowance).

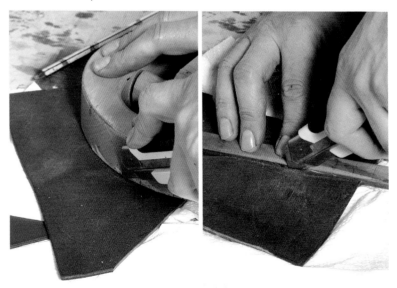

As before: Cut the contour of the leather on the other side with a ruler and French curve template. It should have the same shape as the opposite side.

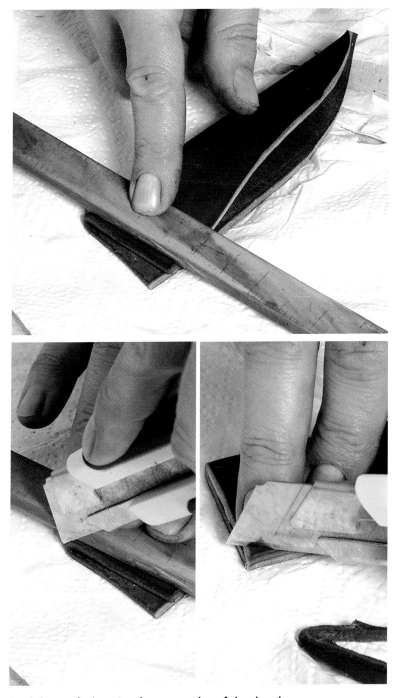

Straight conclusion: Cut the upper edge of the sheath.

After determining the shape of our sheath, smooth the edges so that they are flush. The easiest way to do this is by means of a belt sander—it can also be done manually with abrasive cloth.

Smoothing: Use a belt sander to smooth uneven edges.

Check: The edges should be as straight and level as possible.

This way also works: If you don't have a belt sander you can smooth the edges manually with abrasive cloth.

Important: The outer edges of the leather piece need to be beveled.

Now we cut a welt from the rest of the leather. The welt will be worked into the sheath later on as a protective strip for the blade edge. The welt is skived a bit towards the rear (the upper end of the sheath) so later the seam will not have any visible gradations.

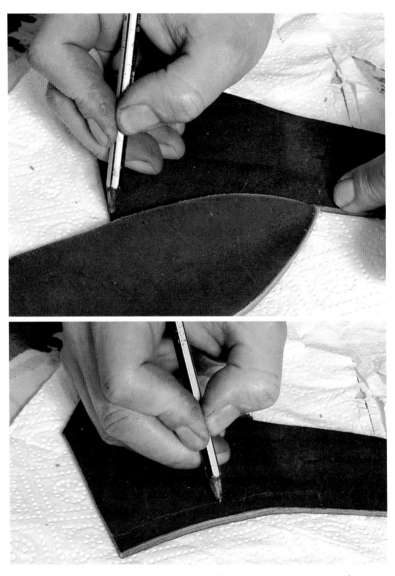

Preparing the welt: From the remainder of the leather, cut a strip with a contour that corresponds to the contour of the sheath along the knife edge.

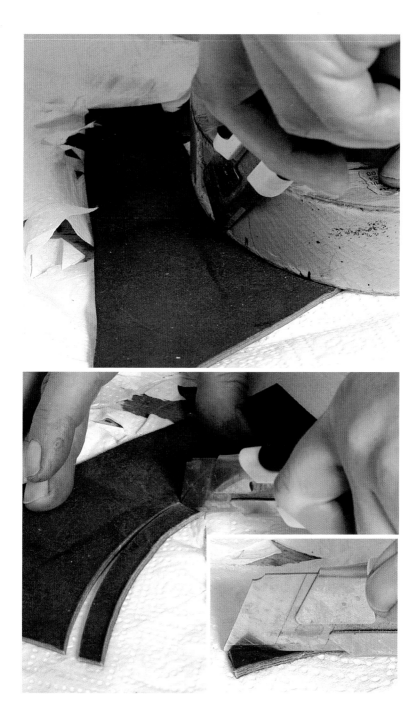

Cutting out: The strip should be as long as the knife sheath. Later it will protect the sheath from being penetrated by the knife's sharp edge.

Fitting end: Cut the tip of the welt off at an angle, so that it fits inside the end of the sheath.

Testing the fit: On the outside the welt follows the contour of the sheath; on the inside it lies against the blade (directly against the knife's edge).

Skiving: the welt is skived at the upper end (towards the sheath opening).

Easier: Skiving is faster with the belt sander.

The reason: Skiving creates a soft transition.

No gradation: Notice the smooth transition towards the upper section.

Now we create a neat groove along the contour of the sheath with an adjustable groover. It enhances the aesthetics and will also serve as a guideline for the seam. Depending on your taste, you can also apply leather dye, which is available in various hues, or you can leave the leather in its natural color.

Drawing a line: The seam is prepared with an adjustable groover.

Personalizing: Now you can emboss the leather with personal logos or patterns.

Wide variety: Many tools for embossing patterns and decorations in leather are available at specialty stores.

Layer of dye: Apply dark brown leather dye, which dries quickly, with a brush.

After the dye has dried (this happens rather quickly), we can fold the sheath to its later shape and put the welt inside, too. The welt should be flush with the edge of the sheath. Fix the alignment with a few clamps and—if everything fits—pour fluid superglue along the leather rim. A few moments later, the clamps can be removed again; the sheath is temporarily held together by the glue.

Critical moment: Fold the sheath, place the welt inside, and fix the whole project in place with several clamps. (Be careful: don't use clamps with sharp edges!)

Preliminary fix: Pour a bit of superglue into the gaps and let it harden briefly. It temporarily provides a sufficiently stable bond.

Prior to further work, shape the edge of the sheath with abrasive cloth (grit P180) and apply leather dye. Then we start sewing: We begin by drilling the holes for sewing. When sewing with yarn, the holes ought to be cut because cut holes are more stable (resistant to tearing) than drilled holes. Here, however, we prefer to work with a 0.078" (2.0 mm) drill bit to achieve somewhat larger holes. Otherwise it would be difficult to pull the leather straps through the holes. The holes are drilled with a consistent separation of 0.118" to 0.196" (3 to 5 mm) between them, depending on personal taste. The size of the drill bit is determined by the width of the harness needle we use for sewing.

Intermediate step: After removing the clamps, go over the edges with an abrasive cloth once more before continuing with the next step.

Simpler and quicker: If you have a belt sander, you have a clear advantage.

Repainting: The reworked edge is painted with leather dye once again.

Boring: Drill the holes for the seam with a 0.078" (2.0 mm) drill bit.

Accuracy is required: The distance between the holes (0.118" to 0.196" [3 to 5 mm]) should be consistent.

Now we cut a leather strap of sufficient length from the spool (the right length is somewhere between 3.28 feet and 5 feet [1 m and 1.50 m]). Attach the strap to the needle (it is clamped in the needle) and off it goes: We sew on the outside each time, from one hole to the next on the other side (see photos). When we have arrived on the other end, we start from the beginning again and pull a second leather strap through the holes, crosswise with respect to the first strap. Thus in the end two straps have been pulled through each hole.

A steady hand is necessary: Clamp the leather strap into the split end of the harness needle, then push the needle through the first hole at the tip of the sheath.

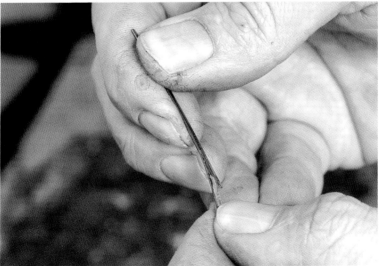

Loop: Pull the leather strap through, lay it back across the edge, then push it through the next hole from the same side as before.

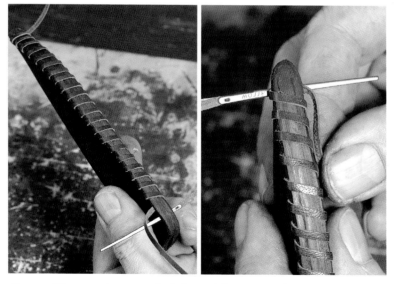

Change: When you have reached the end, leave a small piece of strap behind, then start from the beginning again with a second piece of leather strap, this time from the other side.

Pulling aid: The second round through the same hole is tighter. Tongs or a pair of pliers without teeth are helpful for pulling. But be careful, the leather strap quickly tears apart!

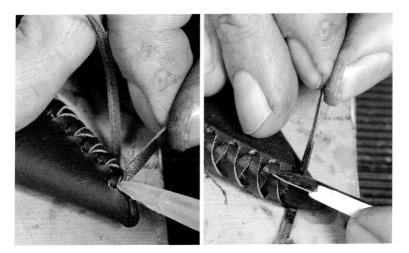

Not so difficult: When both straps have been braided, the ends are pulled tight and fixed with a few drops of superglue. Then they can be cut short.

When this step is completed, drip some superglue onto the last few holes of the seam. The ends of the leather straps can simply be cut off. Don't worry, they will stay fixed.

Now the sheath is fitted to the knife. For this, we (cautiously!) push the knife into the sheath. Since the leather is still soft, it can be easily pierced! When the knife is in the right position, the leather is fitted to the knife manually. Here you also have to take care not to leave any fingernail marks or other scratches.

Sheathing carefully: The knife is carefully placed into the sheath without damaging the leather or piercing it.

Soft massage: The contour of the leather is fitted to the knife. At the transition of blade to handle, an edge has to be created.

In the areas where the leather is stretched, its color gets lighter. Thus we apply another coat of leather dye onto the whole sheath after fitting it to the knife. When the dye has dried, we polish the whole sheath with a soft piece of cloth or a polishing wheel. The sheath opening can best be smoothed with the tip of a stag antler. Rub the edge until it looks smooth and shiny.

Comparing: The blade should reach sufficiently far down inside the sheath, but not too far.

Final dyeing: Once more we apply leather dye and cover the straps.

Insider's tip: Open edges are best polished with the small tip of a stag antler.

Low gloss: After the dye has dried, buff the sheath all around.

Now the only thing remaining is letting the sheath dry. For best results, this should take several days. Leave the knife inside while the sheath dries. Prior to this, however, the knife should be wrapped in plastic wrap so the moisture doesn't damage it. The sheath serves as a reliable home for our knife.

The knife's home is now finished: A simple, but pretty and safe quiver-like sheath.

BELT LOOP OR NOT?

We purposely didn't add a belt loop to the sheath because this sheath is meant to be put inside leather trousers. If you want to attach a belt loop, this has to be done prior to sewing the sheath together. For the belt loop, sew an appropriate piece of leather on to the side of the sheath which faces your body. Here it is also recommended to first fix its position with superglue before cutting the holes for the seam and sewing both parts together with yarn.

LIST OF SUPPLIERS

These suppliers offer tools and materials.

Alpha Knife Supply
(425) 868-5880
chuck@alphaknifesupply.com
www.alphaknifesupply.com

Culpepper & Co.
(828) 524-6842
info@culpepperco.com
www.knifehandles.com

Damasteel AB (Sweden)
(46) 0-293-30600
mail@damasteel.se
www.damasteel.com

Halpern Titanium
(888) 283-8627
info@halperntitanium.com
www.halperntitanium.com/knife.htm

Hawkins Knife Making Supplies
(770) 964-1023
sales@hawkinsknifemakingsupplies.com
www.hawkinsknifemakingsupplies.com

Jantz Supply
(800) 351-8900
jantz@jantzusa.com
www.knifemaking.com

Knife and Gun Finishing Supplies
(800) 972-1192
csinfo@knifeandgun.com
www.knifeandgun.com

NorthCoast Knives
pjp@NorthCoastKnives.com
www.northcoastknives.com

Provision Forge
(541) 846-6755
bladesmith@customknife.com
http://customknife.com

Texas Knifemaker's Supply
(888) 461-8632
sales@texasknife.com
www.texasknife.com

Thompson's Scandinavian Knife Supply
(517) 627-9289
bradjarvis3@comcast.net
www.thompsonknives.com

Tru-Grit Inc. (Canada)
(909) 923-4116
www.trugrit.com

USA Knife Maker Supply
(507) 720-6063
info.usakms@gmail.com
www.usaknifemaker.com

Pocketknife Making for Beginners
Stefan Steigerwald and Peter Fronteddu

Pocketknife Making for Beginners.
Stefan Steigerwald & Peter Fronteddu.
Make your own folding pocketknife with this easy-to-follow guide. Step by step, this instructional manual unfolds the secrets of constructing a slip-joint folding knife, which is held open by spring force and friction. In addition to introducing different variations of this knife style, this guide presents the materials, tools, and technical design skills needed for the project. Diagrams clearly demonstrate the mechanics of your knife and the crucial elements needed to make a properly functioning pocketknife. Detailed step-by-step explanations move from template to finished knife —even beginners can master this project with minimal tool requirements. Once the knife project is complete, you can use the processes in this guide and your own creativity to construct a special knife of your own design.

Size: 6" x 9" • 275+ photos & diagrams • 128 pp.
ISBN: 978-0-7643-3847-2 • spiral bound • $29.99

Basic Knife Making:
From Raw Steel to a Finished Stub Tang Knife.
Ernst G. Siebeneicher-Hellwig and Jürgen Rosinski.
In this book Ernst G. Siebeneicher-Hellwig and Jürgen
Rosinski show the simplest and least expensive ways
to construct a simple forge, make all necessary tools
yourself, forge a stub tang blade from an old automobile
coil spring, and make a complete knife.

Their practical guide dem-
onstrates the most important
theoretical basics and shows
how simple it can be to experience bladesmithing. Each
step is presented in text and
pictures, with a special focus
on forging the blade. Clear
lists of tools and materials
help you through the process.
Practical tips, explanations of
terms, and sketches round out
the volume.

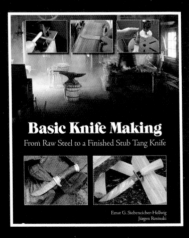

Basic Knife Making
From Raw Steel to a Finished Stub Tang Knife

Ernst G. Siebeneicher-Hellwig
Jürgen Rosinski

Size: 8 1/2" x 11" • 205 color images/10 drawings • 112 pp.
ISBN: 978-0-7643-3508-2 • soft cover • $29.99

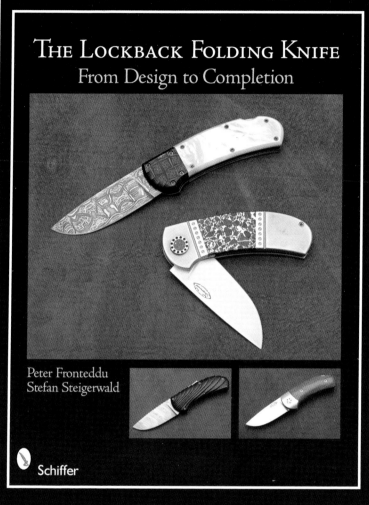

THE LOCKBACK FOLDING KNIFE
From Design to Completion

Peter Fronteddu
Stefan Steigerwald

Schiffer

The Lockback Folding Knife: From Design to Completion.
Peter Fronteddu and Stefan Steigerwald. Take your knifemaking skills to the next level and create your own folding lockback knife. Illustrated instructions and more than 200 color images detail all stages of the knife's construction, from creating a template to making the blade and locking mechanism. With this guide you can tackle the challenging task of constructing a lockback knife and gain the skills necessary to create a lockback knife of your own design.

Size: 8 1/2" x 11" • 236 color images • 112 pp.
ISBN: 978-0-7643-3509-9 • soft cover • $29.99

Sharpening and Knife Making. Jim Watson. Wood carvers understand the feeling of satisfaction, ease and higher quality of carving that comes when using a well sharpened, honed and polished tool. In a process handed down from his grandfather, Jim Watson explains and illustrates sharpening techniques for numerous woodcarving tools and knives of various sizes and shapes including pocket knives and kitchen knives. The necessary materials for proper sharpening are listed and discussed with methods for reconditioning and making your own new knives and tools as well as information on resurfacing the sharpening stones.
By following Jim's instructions and adding a little practice and patience, everyone will be able to achieve and maintain a superior edge, as keen as the piece of steel will allow.

Size: 6" x 9" • 330 b/w photos • 176 pp.
ISBN: 978-0-88740-118-3 • soft cover • $12.99